LET'S FIND OUT ABOUT

BREAD

LET'S FIND OUT ABOUT

BREAD

by Olive Burt

pictures by Mimi Korach

FRANKLIN WATTS, INC.
575 Lexington Avenue, N.Y. 10022

Copyright © 1966 by Franklin Watts, Inc.
Library of Congress Catalog Card Number: 66-18672
Manufactured in the United States of America
5
SBN 531-00009-5

Bread is made from flour, and flour is made
from grain.
In our country, wheat is the most important
grain for making flour.
Most of the wheat we use is winter wheat.
It is planted in the fall and grows through
the winter.

On large wheat farms a motor-driven plow is used to break up the ground and make it ready for the seeds.

On smaller farms, horses may draw the plow while the farmer walks behind to guide it. The wheat seeds are scattered in all directions over the field.

In a short time, green spears pop above the
    ground.
As the wheat grows, seed heads form at the
    top of each stalk.

Each seed head is made up of dozens of small, flat seeds covered with a crisp husk. When the wheat is ripe, it turns a golden brown.

For miles and miles through the middle part of the United States and the flat plains of Canada the golden wheat fields ripple in the summer sunshine.

Now it is time to harvest the wheat.

The farmer uses a large machine called a
   combine.
It is driven like a tractor.

It cuts down the tall stalks of wheat.
As the stalks are cut, they are fed into
   the combine.

There the seeds are separated from the stalks
    and the dry husks.
The seeds are poured into sacks.
The husks are blown away.
The stalks are tied into neat bundles of straw.
This is called threshing.
It is all done by the combine.

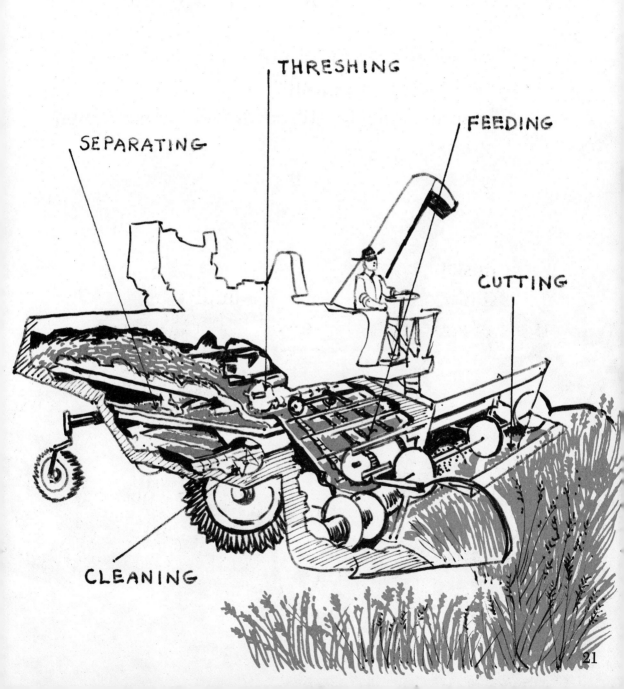

THRESHING

FEEDING

SEPARATING

CUTTING

CLEANING

21

The seeds are stored until they can
be taken to the mill.
The grain may be stored in the farmer's own
granary.

More often it is taken to a grain elevator.
This is a tall, narrow building near railroad
    tracks or a ship dock.
From these tall buildings the grain can be
    poured into railroad cars or ships to be
    taken to the mill.

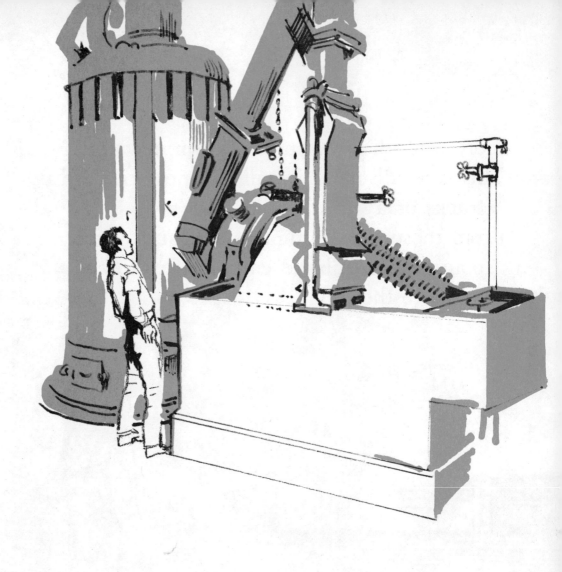

At the mill the grain is put through machines
that wash away all the dirt and dust.
Then it is run between great iron rollers that
crush the seeds.

Now the tough, yellow outer hull is blown
away by air currents.
The hulls are caught and used for cattle feed.
They are called bran.

The white, inner part of the seed is crushed
again and sifted.
Often minerals and vitamins are added to
replace those lost with the hulls.
The wheat is now good, white flour, ready
for the baker.

Sometimes the whole grain is ground into
    whole wheat flour.
This flour contains all the parts of the wheat
    kernels.

Most bread in our country is made in large
   bakeries.
There everything is done by machines.
Machines weigh and measure the flour.
Water, sugar, salt, milk powder, vitamins,
   minerals, and yeast are added to make a
   dough.

The yeast makes the dough swell up and
   become light.
This is called rising.

KEEP TEMPERATURE
AND HUMIDITY
CONSTANT

When the dough is ready, machines cut and
shape it into loaves.
These are put on a moving tray-oven and
baked.
The heat makes the crust form and turn a
golden brown.

WRAPPER
OVERWRAPS SEALS
CODES AND PRICES
EACH LOAF
AUTOMATICALLY

After the bread is baked and cooled,
  machines slice and wrap it.
Then it is sent to markets and grocery stores.
Bread is also made in neighborhood bakeries
  and in the home.

Wheat is not the only grain used for making
   bread.
Oats, rye, barley, rice, and corn also make
   good bread.
On the shelves of a market or bakery we find
   many kinds of bread.

41

There are the sliced and wrapped white and
  whole wheat loaves.
There are dark rye breads called pumper-
  nickel and there are regular rye breads.
There are muffins, doughnuts, buns, and
  crackers.
There are partly baked rolls which need only
  to be browned in the oven at home.
There are frozen loaves to be baked at home.

There are packaged mixes for muffins, corn
   bread, and brown bread.
These need only water or milk to be added.
Then they are ready for baking.
All these save time and work in preparing the
   many kinds of bread the American family
   uses.

For breakfast we eat toast or muffins or
pancakes or waffles.

Our lunch may be a sandwich or a hamburger or hot dog on a bun.

For dinner, sliced bread or hot rolls or biscuits are on the table.

No other food is eaten so often by so many people all over the world.

Every year each of us eats about two bushels
   of wheat made into flour.
A growing boy or girl needs six to eight
   slices of bread a day.
Bread with cheese or milk is an almost per-
   fect food.
That is why bread is often called "the Staff
   of Life."

51